VLADIMIR NABOKOV

A PICTORIAL BIOGRAPHY

Compiled & Edited by Ellendea Proffer

Ardis, Ann Arbor

Ardis Publishers
2901 Heatherway
Ann Arbor, Michigan 48104

Library of Congress Cataloging-in-Publication Data

Vladimir Nabokov : a pictorial biography / edited by Ellendea Proffer.
p.   cm.
ISBN 0-87501-078-4 (cloth : alk. paper)
1. Nabokov, Vladimir Vladimirovich, 1899-1977—Pictorial works.
2. Authors, Russian—20th century—Pictorial works. I. Proffer, Ellendea.
PG3476.N3Z92   1991
813'.54—dc20
[B]   91-14123
                                           CIP

Jacket & Book Design by Ross Teasley

ACKNOWLEDGMENTS

I wish to thank Véra and Dmitri Nabokov for allowing me to go through the photograph archives in Montreux, and for their warm hospitality as well.

Permission was graciously given to reproduce the works of the following photographers: Yves Cornaro; Maclean Dameron; Gertrude Fehr; Philippe Halsman; Joffé, Courtesy of *Vogue.* Copyright © 1947 (renewed 1975) by The Condé Nast Publication Inc.; R. T. Kahn; Patellani; Elena Seibert; Clayton Smith; Horst Tappe; and Jean Waldis.

Special thanks is due to Yvonne Halsman for her encouragement, and to D. Barton Johnson for last minute corrections.

INTRODUCTION

Photographs do indeed tell a story, but the story they tell can just as easily be false as true; nevertheless, many pictures of the same subject taken over a lifetime do, in the end, convey something not always accessible to logic. It has been my fate to be involved in the compilation of several pictorial biographies of Russian writers, and each experience was profoundly different. Mikhail Bulgakov was fascinating-a different face in almost every shot, all conveying tension, however. Nikolai Evreinov, logically enough for an avant-garde director, was theatrical in every gesture and seemed to be having a good time no matter what the circumstance. Easily the most harrowing was the one devoted to Marina Tsvetaeva, as great a poet as Nabokov was a prose writer. Not only did the poet end as a suicide, but the Leningrad collector who gave me the photographs (which he had collected over a lifetime), also committed suicide just before he was to receive a copy of the book. As I worked on arranging all the pictures of Tsvetaeva, I found myself getting disturbed even when dealing with her better years. Her character, which was, unfortunately, her fate, seemed to jump out at me from each picture, as if to say: This will all end very badly.

With Nabokov it is quite a different experience, although looking at the lost beauty and immense wealth of his childhood one might have reason to expect a sense of sadness, if not bitterness. It is a commonplace of Nabokov criticism that this early loss fueled his genius and sharpened his most powerful tool, memory, but as I went through these pictures in the archives in Montreux I was happy to be confirmed in the impression I had received on first meeting him that he had not only survived this overwhelming loss, he had gone on to flourish-even before the publication of *Lolita* at last made him financially stable.

This book is really a visual accompaniment to the entire text of *Speak, Memory,* and the biographical sections of Brian Boyd's two-volume study, but even without the sort of elucidation these works provide, much may be deduced from the photographs alone.

The world of Nabokov's childhood, so vital to the understanding of his later development, is represented fairly fully. The three country estates, the enormous resources represented by all those relatives banqueting alfresco, the emphasis on the country life-as opposed to the life in the Petersburg mansion-all of this is revealing. More significant, of course, are his remarkable parents, the beautiful, high-strung mother who would do everything to encourage the sort of genius her son seemed to possess from the start, and his father, that very secure male figure who would represent the essence of honor to his son.

Nabokov was the first child, and the life-long favorite of his parents. They recognized his abilities, and both of them gave unstinting support to him when he began his literary career. In the pictures of Nabokov at age nine we can already see the remarkable self-assurance which will be his for life. It is easy to imagine this child growing up and writing to Edmund Wilson: "Once [and] for all you should tell yourself that in these questions of prosody-no matter the language involved-you are wrong and I am right, always." He will need that confidence, that ability to believe in himself under the most trying circumstances, even if at times he is wrong (and refuses to admit it). This indulged child will be tested severely.

In Russia Nabokov seemed a bit of an Englishman, and was independent in his opinions from an early age. In England, where he attended Cambridge after the Revolution (his mother sold some jewels so that he might be educated), his friends appear to have been mostly Russian, and in Berlin he lived an entirely Russian existence. In America he was, of course, a European intellectual. Finally, in Switzerland, he was a blend of all of these things-but never Swiss. This position outside of categories seems to have suited him well; he was never a willing member of a club, and, indeed, in the archives there were remarkably few photographs of Nabokov with other writers. In terms of his art Russia and America appear to have inspired his best works, but there is no doubt that his heart lay with the Russia-and the Russian-of his childhood and youth. The images of what surrounded him in childhood make it easy to understand why he appeared to refuse to make a real home ever again, preferring temporary quarters in rented apartments, houses whose owners were away, and, ultimately, a hotel suite. He had lost a home, a country, and a world, and was obviously determined never to become so attached to a place again.

The handsome young Russian from Petersburg is still visible in the Cambridge pictures, but by the time we get to Berlin, the strain of the battle for existence is showing. Memoirists who knew him in this period often comment that Nabokov had a grand indifference to food and drink, but another explanation suggests itself. In some of these pictures he appears gaunt rather than slim, like someone who is not getting quite enough food. Véra wears this look as well (whereas the young Dmitri always appears well fed). In any case, watching Nabokov eat in later years, it was clear to me that in this, as in everything else, he was an authentic sensualist.

We know from many sources just how hard existence became for the Nabokov family in the 1930s, but the pictures from that period show other sides (the arrival of Dmitri produces a few photos in which Nabokov actually smiles). The pictures of Nabokov working on his writing show someone who does not appear to think that he is writing for the small audience of the Russian emigration, where there were so few readers and precious little understanding of his sort of writing, although, it is true, what understanding there was came from remarkable people. He was confident that he belonged to the tradition of Russian literature, and that his contribution was substantial. However, he never expected that one day he would have an audience in the Soviet Union. Indeed, he had made a conscious decision to give up the hope that his Russia would ever be restored, and this must have been a terrible moment. For a brief period the emigration had seemed a rich, stimulating milieu, but very quickly a number of factors, including the rise of Hitler, caused the audience to shrink.

It is hard to overestimate the difficulty most writers would have had in this situation. Even harder to appreciate is the difficulty of what he did next, when he saw that he would have to get his family to America or England if they were to survive: switch languages after having developed a brilliant new style in Russian. The photograph on the cover of this book is from this period: Nabokov has written a masterpiece, *The Gift*, in Russian, but he is beginning his first novel in English, *The Real Life of Sebastian Knight*, and will soon board a boat for America.

The first pictures in America seem wildly discontinuous with what has gone before. The elegant Véra, the thin, European Nabokov, the lanky Dmitri . . . in Salt Lake City, going across country hunting butterflies on the way to a job. But gradually Nabokov starts to fit into the new landscape, becoming much more the image of a man of letters, as in the photo at Wellesley where he appears as a slightly heavy faun reclining near those frankly fascinated Wellesley girls.

And then–fame and fortune, and something like a return to his and Véra's wealthy childhoods, living in the Montreux-Palace Hotel as permanent residents. Now the photographs are of a literary lion at the peak of his fame. But even here Nabokov could not quite resist making fun of his own august image, and I have included one of Philippe Halsman's photographs by the Montreux pool to show that side of him.

Nabokov was a very physical man. He was athletic when young and continued to go on butterfly collecting expeditions well into old age. When my husband and I first met the Nabokovs in 1969, he had just been on such an expedition, and I remember being struck by how tall he was, and how strong his legs looked in his shorts. This was during the very same period when Soviet intellectuals imagined him looking something like Kafka, and thought that his literary snobbery indicated a very delicate constitution.

The Nabokov that we met was witty, funny, and curious about everything. This was the comfortable Nabokov, relaxed with two young (and quite unimportant) scholars. There was a great freedom in his conversation, and occasionally sharp-witted Véra would warn him not to be too frank. She was very beautiful–more so than when young–and had a very good sense of humor, but vastly less trust in people than her husband did. Their bond was immediately sensed, and I think the many pictures of them together in this book convey it quite well. Nabokov's deepest feelings were reserved for his family, his wife and child in particular, and in a sense, they lived in a world of their own. His love for, and pride in Dmitri is everywhere evident, but how much that love was returned is especially clear in the last picture taken of them together, a very personal picture which I hesitated to include, but which in the end I decided was necessary to my conception of this book–and its subject's character.

Véra, of course, is the "you" addressed so often in Nabokov's fiction, always his first reader, and a demanding critic. She was clearly a full partner in all ways, taking care of all practical arrangements (including negotiations with publishers), and making it possible for him to devote himself completely to his work–or should I say play, for that was the feeling I had. A sense of joy in the world is to be found all through Nabokov's works, and when I look at the photographs of him at work writing, I see someone absorbed in an endeavor which gives him the deepest satisfaction.

When in the 1960s we, and others like us, told Nabokov that he had been wrong to assume he had no readers in the Soviet Union, that on the contrary, he was a cult figure among the intelligentsia, it was pleasant for him to hear, I think, but it was too late: his Russia, the Russia of these pictures was gone forever. Not that he did not have interest or concern for his native land, he did, but one felt that he had emigrated long ago to his real country, the country of literature.

Ellendea Proffer
Ann Arbor, 1991

A NABOKOV CHRONOLOGY

(The following is not meant to be either a bibliography or an exhaustive description of Vladimir Nabokov's life. It is meant only as a framework within which to place the photographs in this book.)

1899   April 23: Birth of Vladimir Vladimirovich Nabokov (hereafter referred to as VN) to Elena Rukavishnikov and Vladimir Dmitrievich Nabokov in St. Petersburg.

1908   V. D. Nabokov, a member of the First Duma, is sent to prison for three months for signing a political manifesto.

1911   VN enters the Tenishev School.

1914   VN writes his first poem.

1916   VN's first book of poetry is published: *Poems (Stikhi)*. (All works will be cited in English, although they are written in Russian until 1941, at which point VN switches to writing in English.)

1917   V. D. Nabokov accepts a post in the Provisional Government after the Revolution.

1917   November 2: VN and his brother Sergei leave St. Petersburg for the Crimea, where the family was offered refuge on a friend's estate. His mother and sisters follow soon after.

1917   November 23: V. D. Nabokov is briefly imprisoned by the Bolsheviks in Petrograd. On the 29th he leaves for the south after narrowly escaping yet another arrest. In the Crimea he becomes a member of the Crimean Regional Government.

1919   April 2: As the Red Army advances, the government leaders are ordered evacuated. The Nabokov family leaves on a ship from Sebastopol for Constantinople.

1919-22   VN attends Trinity College, Cambridge. His family is temporarily settled in England.

1920   August: The Nabokov family moves to Berlin, where V. D. Nabokov will become editor of the Russian newspaper *Rul'*.

1922   March 28: V. D. Nabokov is fatally shot during an assassination attempt on the politician Miliukov by right-wing monarchists.

1922   June: VN receives his degree from Cambridge in French and Russian.

1922-23   VN lives with his family in Berlin. He publishes two collections of poetry and his first chess problem.

1923   May 8: VN meets his future wife, Véra Slonim, at a charity costume ball in Berlin.

1923   Elena Nabokov and her daughter Elena move to Prague, where she is offered a government pension as the widow of V. D. Nabokov.

1924   VN completes his first play, *The Tragedy of Mr. Morn*.

1925   April 15: VN and Véra Slonim marry in Berlin.

1925   VN writes *Mary*, his first novel.

1926   *Mary* is published in Berlin.

1927   *The Man from the USSR*, his second play, is produced in Berlin.

1928   *King, Queen, Knave*, his second novel, is written and published.

1929   VN and Véra travel to Paris and then to the Eastern Pyrenees to hunt butterflies. VN writes *The Defense* which begins to come out in the Parisian journal *Contemporary Annals* (and continues into 1930), and publishes the collection *The Return of Chorb: Stories and Poems*.

1930   VN publishes *The Eye* in *Contemporary Annals*.

1931   *Glory* begins to come out in *Contemporary Annals* (and continues into 1932), as does *Laughter in the Dark* (which continues into 1933).

1932   *Glory* is published in book form in Paris.

1933   Works on *The Gift. Laughter in the Dark* comes out in book form in Berlin.

1934   *Despair* comes out in journal form. Dmitri Nabokov is born on May 10.

1935-36   *Invitation to a Beheading* comes out in *Contemporary Annals*.

1936   Publication of *Despair* in book form.

1937   *Despair* comes out in English in London. Nabokov sees his mother for the last time in Prague.

1937-38   *Laughter in the Dark* comes out in English in London.

    The Gift comes out in the journal *Contemporary Annals*, minus the fourth chapter which was censored by the editors.

    The Nabokovs move to France and spend time in Menton and other locations in the south of France, as well as in Paris.

1938   *Invitation to a Beheading* comes out in book form. A book containing *The Eye* and twelve short stories is published in Paris.

    In December VN begins his first novel in English, *The Real Life of Sebastian Knight*. This marks the moment when he decides that he will have to change languages to survive, either in England or America, since the émigré audience has shrunk and the political situation in Europe is very dangerous for a liberal Russian émigré—with a Jewish wife.

1940   May: VN, Véra and their son leave France for the United States. VN renews friendship with Professor

Michael Karpovich of Harvard, who will be important for his future academic career, and meets Edmund Wilson, who will be instrumental in publishing Nabokov's works in America.

1941   Nabokov's first novel composed in English, *The Real Life of Sebastian Knight*, is published in the US.

The family makes the first of what will become annual butterfly-hunting trips across the country. VN teaches creative writing at Stanford during the summer.

VN receives an offer to teach at Wellesley College; at first the family lives in the college town in Massachusetts, then moves to Cambridge. VN begins to work part-time at Harvard's Museum of Comparative Zoology, an association which will continue until 1948.

1942   Beginning of VN's long association with *The New Yorker*.

1944   *Nikolai Gogol* published.

1945   The Nabokovs become American citizens (and remain so). VN's brother, Sergei, dies in a German concentration camp.

1947   *Bend Sinister* is published in English.

1948   VN moves to Cornell University in Ithaca, New York, where he receives the rank of professor.

1951   *Conclusive Evidence* is published in English.

1952   *The Gift* is published in book form in Russian for the first time in New York.

1954   *Other Shores* (a Russian version, with many changes, of the English memoirs) is published.

1955   September 15: *Lolita* is published in English in Paris.

December 25: Graham Greene chooses *Lolita* as one of the books of the year for *The Sunday Times* of London.

1956   *Spring in Fialta*, a collection of stories, is published in Russian.

December 20: French government bans *Lolita* and 25 other books in English from Olympia Press.

1957   *Pnin*, VN's first popular English novel, is published.

1958   August 18: The New York edition of *Lolita* is published.

September 28: *Lolita* is in first place on *The New York Times* bestseller list.

1959   Publication in English of *Invitation to a Beheading*, *Spring in Fialta*, and *Poems*.

VN resigns from Cornell and makes his first trip to Europe since 1940, for a reunion with family and friends.

1960   VN returns to the US and goes to California to write the screenplay for Stanley Kubrick's film of *Lolita* (the screenplay will not be used).

French and Italian publication of *Lolita*.

1961   The Nabokovs settle in the Montreux-Palace Hotel in Montreux, Switzerland to be near their son, who is making a career in opera in Italy, and VN's sister. At first they assume it is a temporary move.

1962   *Pale Fire* is published.

The Nabokovs return to the United States for the première of the movie of *Lolita* on June 13 in New York. VN is on the cover of *Newsweek*.

1963   *The Gift* is published in English.

1964   *The Defense* is published in English.

The translation of *Eugene Onegin* with extensive commentaries is published in English.

VN returns to the US to give a reading at Harvard and meet with his publishers.

1965   *The Eye* is published in English.

1966   *Speak, Memory* is published in English.

1967   VN's Russian translation of *Lolita* is published in New York.

1968   *King, Queen, Knave* is published in English.

1969   *Ada* is published. VN receives cover story in *Time*.

1970   *Mary* is published in English.

1971   *Glory* is published in English.

1972   Publication of *Transparent Things*.

1973   Publication of *Strong Opinions*.

1974   *Look at the Harlequins!* is published.

1977   July 2: VN dies in Montreux, Switzerland.

NABOKOV

A PICTORIAL BIOGRAPHY

RUSSIA

Иванъ Александровичъ
НАБОКОВЪ

GENERAL IVAN ALEXANDROVICH NABOKOV

(1787-1852), GREAT-GRANDUNCLE OF VN.

A HERO WHO FOUGHT NAPOLEON, HE MARRIED

THE SISTER OF IVAN PUSHCHIN, A DECEMBRIST.

THE NABOKOV COAT OF ARMS.

VN'S MATERNAL GRANDFATHER,

IVAN VASILIEVICH RUKAVISHNIKOV

(1841-1901).

VN'S PATERNAL GRANDFATHER,

DMITRI NIKOLAEVICH NABOKOV (1826-1904),

MINISTER OF JUSTICE UNDER TSARS ALEXANDER II

AND ALEXANDER III. ST. PETERSBURG, c. 1880.

VN'S PATERNAL GRANDMOTHER,

MARIA NABOKOV, BORN

BARONESS VON KORFF (1842-1926),

WITH VN'S FATHER.

VN'S MATERNAL GRANDMOTHER,

OLGA NIKOLAEVNA RUKAVISHNIKOV (1845-1901),

WITH VN'S MOTHER.

VN'S FATHER, VLADIMIR
DMITRIEVICH NABOKOV
(1870-1922), (FAR
RIGHT) WITH HIS THREE
BROTHERS,
c. 1885.

VN'S MATERNAL GRANDMOTHER, c. 1885.

VN'S PATERNAL GRANDMOTHER.

VYRA, THE SUMMER ESTATE WHICH HAD COME FROM VN'S MATERNAL GRANDFATHER

IVAN VASILIEVICH RUKAVISHNIKOV, AND WHICH WAS TO REPRESENT THE ESSENCE OF CHILDHOOD FOR THE WRITER.

Левицкій   Ст. Петербургъ

1895

VN'S MOTHER, ELENA IVANOVNA RUKAVISHNIKOV (1876-1939), WITH HER MOTHER, OLGA NIKOLAEVNA. ST. PETERSBURG, 1895.

GATHERING MUSHROOMS AT VYRA.
VN'S MOTHER AND GRANDMOTHER
ARE HOLDING HANDS.

ELENA NABOKOV AND HER BROTHER
("UNCLE RUKA"), VASILY IVANOVICH
RUKAVISHNIKOV (1874-1916).

VN'S FATHER, V. D. NABOKOV, WITH HIS

COUSIN, CATHERINE DANZAS, DRESSED FOR

A COSTUME BALL (SHE IS A GEORGIAN

WOMAN, HE A TOREADOR).

SOUVENIR OF A COSTUME BALL AT

BATOVO, AUGUST, 1889.

VN'S MOTHER,

ELENA RUKAVISHNIKOV.

ST. PETERSBURG, c. 1898.

A CEREMONIAL BANQUET AT VYRA.

ELENA RUKAVISHNIKOV AND V. D. NABOKOV, FIFTH AND SIXTH FROM RIGHT.

FIFTH FROM LEFT IS VN'S MATERNAL GRANDFATHER, IVAN VASILIEVICH RUKAVISHNIKOV,

OWNER OF THE VYRA AND ROZHESTVENO (LATER ROZHDESTVENO) ESTATES.

A FAMILY PICNIC. V. D. NABOKOV (BACK TO CAMERA), WITH ELENA IVANOVNA IN WHITE HAT.

VN'S MOTHER (FAR RIGHT), PLAYING TENNIS AT ROZHESTVENO WITH HER BROTHER.

A GATHERING AT VYRA TO CELEBRATE THE ENGAGEMENT OF VN'S PARENTS, STANDING THIRD AND FOURTH FROM LEFT. AT THE HEAD OF THE TABLE, FAR

RIGHT, SITS VN'S MATERNAL GRANDMOTHER, OLGA RUKAVISHNIKOV; TO HER LEFT, TURNED TO THE CAMERA IS MARIA NABOKOV, HIS PATERNAL

GRANDMOTHER. NEXT TO HER, PROFILE TO THE CAMERA, IS HIS GRANDFATHER, IVAN RUKAVISHNIKOV.

VN'S PARENTS AT VYRA, 1900.

VN IN 1901, TWO YEARS OLD.

VN AND HIS MOTHER.

VN AND HIS BROTHER SERGEI. BIARRITZ, DECEMBER, 1901.

THE AVENUE OF OAKS, VYRA.

ABBAZIA (NOW, OPATJE, YUGOSLAVIA) — VILLA NEPTUNE, WHERE VN GOES AT AGE FIVE AND FIRST EXPERIENCES LONGING FOR VYRA.

SEE *SPEAK, MEMORY*. (THIS PICTURE TAKEN c. 1920.)

VN AND HIS FATHER.

ST. PETERSBURG, 1906.

VN WITH HIS MOTHER AND

HER BROTHER, VASSILY RUKAVISHNIKOV.

VYRA.

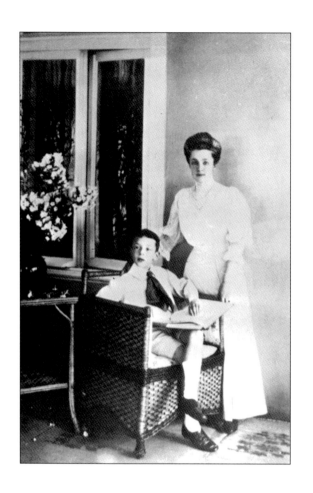

VN AND HIS MOTHER.

VYRA, 1907.

VN WITH A BUTTERFLY BOOK.

VYRA, 1907.

ELENA NABOKOV AND HER CHILDREN,

LEFT TO RIGHT: SERGEI, OLGA, ELENA AND VN,

1907.

SERGEI, VN, AND MLLE. MIAUTON,

THEIR FRENCH GOVERNESS,

1907.

A FAMILY GATHERING IN AUGUST, 1908, AFTER V. D. NABOKOV WAS RELEASED FROM PRISON. VN'S PARENTS ARE

STANDING. MARIA NABOKOV, VN'S MATERNAL GRANDMOTHER, IS SEATED HOLDING HIS SISTERS, ELENA AND OLGA; VN

AND HIS BROTHER SERGEI SIT ON EITHER SIDE OF PRASKOVIA NIKOLAEVNA TARNOVSKY, AUNT OF VN'S MOTHER.

SERGEI (LEFT) AND VN AT BATOVO, SUMMER 1909, AGED NINE AND TEN.

ELENA NABOKOV AND HER SONS.

BAD KISSINGEN, GERMANY, 1910.

VN IN BERLIN, READY TO GO SKATING.

VN'S MOTHER AND HER BROTHER, VASSILY

RUKAVISHNIKOV, AT HIS CHATEAU AT

PAU, BASSES PYRÉNÉES. OCTOBER, 1913.

PORTRAIT OF ELENA NABOKOV BY

LEON BAKST, 1910.

(ORIGINAL IN THE COLLECTION OF

THE RUSSIAN MUSEUM, LENINGRAD)

THE NABOKOVS' HOUSE IN
ST. PETERSBURG ON MORSKAYA STREET
(NOW HERZEN STREET).
(PHOTO: PROF. S. KOSMAN, 1964)

WINDOW DETAIL OF
THE HOUSE.

THE RUKAVISHNIKOVS' CRYPT

NEAR THE OREDEZH RIVER.

ROZHESTVENO

MANOR, 1967.

VN'S FIRST LOVE, VALENTINA SHULGIN

(TAMARA OF *SPEAK, MEMORY*), 1916.

(*IZVESTIIA*)

VN, 1916.

EVA LUBRZYNSKA, ONE OF VN'S MAIN

ROMANTIC INTERESTS FROM 1917 TO 1920.

THE NABOKOV CHILDREN FIVE MONTHS BEFORE THEY

WERE TO LEAVE RUSSIA.

LEFT TO RIGHT: VN, KIRILL, OLGA, SERGEI AND ELENA.

NOVEMBER, 1918.

YURI RAUSCH VON

TRAUBENBERG, IN 1917.

VN'S COUSIN AND BEST

FRIEND. HE WOULD DIE

DURING THE CIVIL WAR.

EXILE

VN AS AN UNDERGRADUATE AT TRINITY COLLEGE.

CAMBRIDGE, NOVEMBER, 1919.

VN AT CAMBRIDGE, 1920.   VN AT CAMBRIDGE, 1920.

VN AND ROBERT DE CALRY PUNTING ON THE CAM. CAMBRIDGE, 1920-21.

CAMBRIDGE, 1920-21.

VN ON THE CAM, 1920.

VN MOUNTAIN CLIMBING IN SWITZERLAND WITH HIS

CAMBRIDGE FRIEND ROBERT DE CALRY. DECEMBER, 1921.

VN (SECOND FROM LEFT) AND DE CALRY (FAR RIGHT), JUNE, 1922.

VN PLAYING TENNIS WITH HIS FIANCÉE

SVETLANA SIEWERT AND

HER SISTER TATIANA.

BERLIN, 1922.

V. D. NABOKOV IN BERLIN, FEBRUARY 17, 1922. ON MARCH 28, 1922, HE WOULD BE KILLED BY RIGHT-WING RUSSIAN

MONARCHIST ASSASSINS DURING AN ATTEMPT ON THE LIFE OF PAVEL MILIUKOV.

VN THE SUMMER AFTER HIS FATHER'S DEATH,

AT THE HOME OF SVETLANA SIEWERT, 1922.

TENNIS IN BERLIN, VN SECOND FROM LEFT. c. 1922-23.

VN IN BERLIN, c. 1925.

BERLIN, c. 1923.

VN IN MAY, 1923, SOON AFTER MEETING VÉRA SLONIM (ON MAY 8). HERE HE IS IN THE SOUTH OF FRANCE WORKING AS A FARMHAND

FOR THE SUMMER AT DOMAINE-BEAULIEU, NEAR TOULON, ON AN ESTATE OWNED BY RUSSIAN FRIENDS OF THE FAMILY.

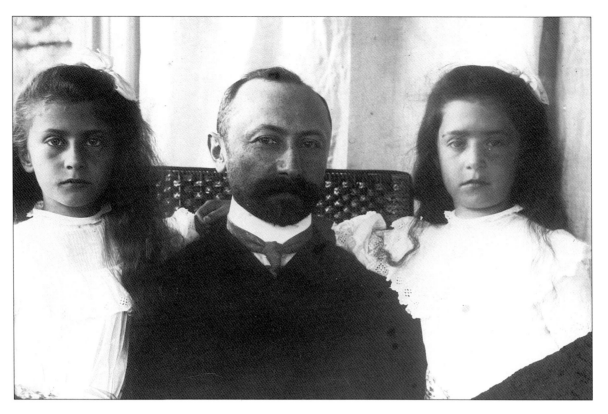

VÉRA EVSEEVNA SLONIM (1902-91), LEFT, WITH HER FATHER, EVSEI (1865-1928),

AND SISTER, SOFIA.

VÉRA IN BERLIN, OCTOBER, 1923.

VÉRA SLONIM AND VN. BERLIN, 1923.

VN IN THE 1920s.

VN AND VÉRA. BERLIN-CHARLOTTENBURG, c. 1924.

VN, 1926.

VÉRA, MID-1920s.

VN WITH HIS STUDENT, ALEXANDER SAK. CONSTANCE, GERMANY, 1925.

ELIZAVETA KAMINKA (LYALYA), HER DOG DOLLY, VÉRA AND VN. BERLIN, LATE 1920s.

VN (SECOND FROM LEFT, FRONT ROW) WITH THE CAST OF HIS PLAY *THE MAN FROM*

THE USSR. THE PREMIÈRE TOOK PLACE ON APRIL 1, 1927, IN BERLIN.

VÉRA AND VN (FAR LEFT) WITH THE BROMBERG CHILDREN AND

FRIENDS FROM THE TENNIS CLUB IN BERLIN.

RÜGEN, BAY OF POMERANIA, AUGUST, 1927.

VN, LATE 1920s.

VÉRA, c. EARLY 1930s.

VN WORKING ON *THE DEFENSE* AT A HOTEL IN LE BOULOU, EAST PYRENEES, FEBRUARY 27, 1929.

SEE *SPEAK, MEMORY* FOR VN'S WONDERFUL CAPTION.

VN AT AGE 30.

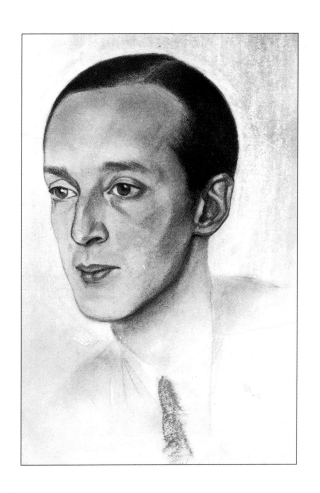

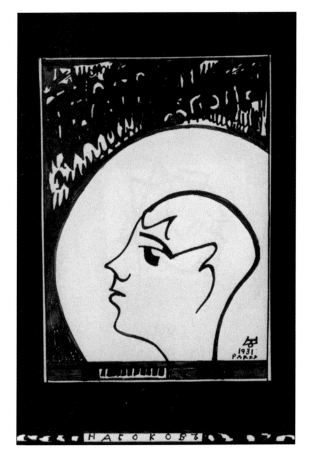

A 1933 PORTRAIT OF VN

BY MAGDA NACHMAN-ACHARIYA.

A 1931 PORTRAIT OF VN

BY ALEKSEI REMIZOV

(FROM THE THOMAS P. WHITNEY COLLECTION).

VN'S INSCRIPTION READS: "MOTHER IN HER 12TH YEAR OF EXILE. PRAGUE." 1931.

VN'S BROTHER

KIRILL, 1929.

(LEFT TO RIGHT): SAVELY (SABA) KYANDZHUNTSEV, NICOLAS NABOKOV, IRINA KYANDZHUNTSEV, VN, AND NATALIA NABOKOV. PARIS, 1932.

VN (SITTING) IN 1932, WITH THE MEMBERS OF THE SOCCER TEAM

OF BERLIN'S RUSSIAN SPORTING CLUB.

VN (FACING CAMERA DIRECTLY, ON RIGHT)

AT THE REUNION OF TENISHEV SCHOOL ALUMNI, BERLIN, c. 1933.

VN, HIS SON DMITRI (b. MAY, 1934) AND VÉRA.

VN ON A BERLIN STREET, 1934.

VN AND DMITRI.

THE NABOKOV FAMILY. BERLIN, SUMMER OF 1935.

VN AND GEORGE HESSEN, HIS BEST
FRIEND, SON OF JOSEPH HESSEN, EDITOR
OF *RUL'*.

ELENA SIKORSKI, VN'S SISTER, WITH HER
HUSBAND, VSEVOLOD SIKORSKI (1896-1958).

A SMILING VN WITH DMITRI.

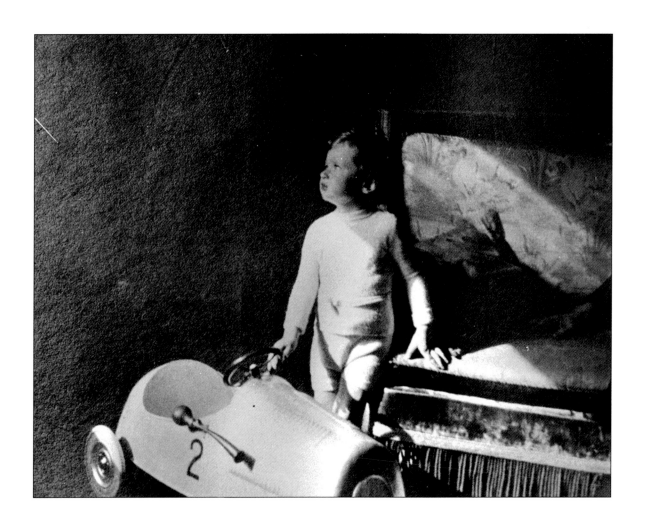

DMITRI. BERLIN, 1936.

VN IN BERLIN, 1936.

THIS WAS HIS FAVORITE PICTURE OF HIMSELF.

NABOKOV IN THE WORLD OF LITERARY PARIS, APRIL, 1937,

AT THE VILLA OF HENRY CHURCH, WHO SPONSORED THE JOURNAL *MESURES*.

LEFT TO RIGHT: HENRI MICHAUX, VN, ADRIENNE MONNIER, SYLVIA BEACH

(STANDING BEHIND), GERMAINE PAULHAN (SEATED), MICHEL LEIRIS (STANDING),

MME. CHURCH, JEAN PAULHAN, HENRY CHURCH (SEATED).

(PHOTO: GISÉLE FREUND)

THE SAME GROUP, VN STANDING SECOND FROM LEFT.

(PHOTO: GISÈLE FREUND)

MENTON, SOUTH OF FRANCE, DECEMBER, 1937.

VN IN MENTON, 1937-38.

VN IN MENTON, 1937-38.

THE TWO BUTTERFLIES VN DISCOVERED IN JULY, 1938 IN THE ALPES MARITIMES AND NAMED

PLEBEJUS (LYSANDRA) CORMION NABOKOV.

VN IN 1938.

VN, PARIS, 1939.

VÉRA'S FAVORITE PHOTOGRAPH OF HIM.

THE PHOTOGRAPH OF VÉRA AND DMITRI ON THEIR NANSEN PASSPORT.

PARIS, 1940.

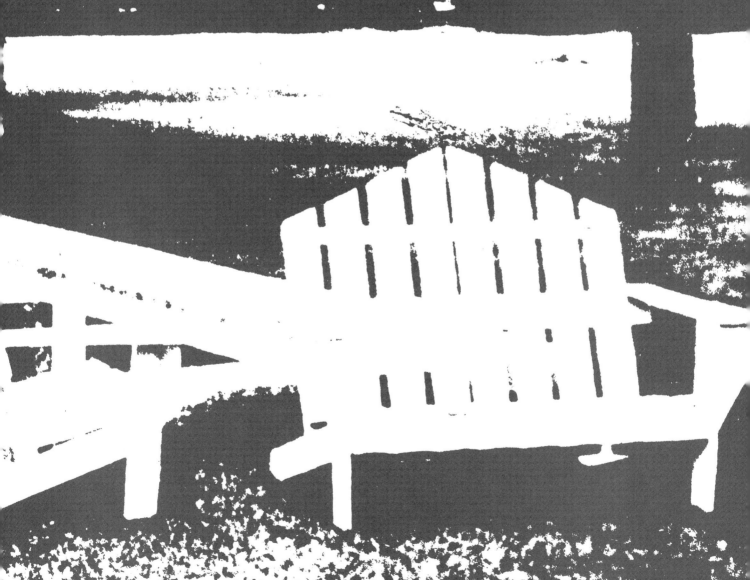

AMERICA

THE NABOKOVS' FIRST BUTTERFLY-COLLECTING

SUMMER IN AMERICA, 1941. THEY WERE DRIVEN BY

VN'S STUDENT, DOROTHY LEUTHOLD, FROM NEW

YORK TO PALO ALTO, CALIFORNIA.

SUMMER, 1943. THE NABOKOVS IN SALT LAKE CITY.

VN AND VÉRA AT WELLESLEY, c. 1944.

DMITRI AND VN, WELLESLEY, c. 1944.

VN AND HIS WELLESLEY STUDENTS, c. 1945-46.

SUMMER 1946, AT A NEW HAMPSHIRE LODGE.

VN WORKING AT HARVARD'S MUSEUM OF COMPARATIVE ZOOLOGY, 1947.

(PHOTO: JOFFÉ)

VÉRA AND VN AT CORNELL, c. 1954.

DMITRI AND VN.

NABOKOV AT CORNELL, c. 1955.

(PHOTO: CLAYTON SMITH)

VN READING *PNIN*.

CORNELL, 1958.

(PHOTO: MACLEAN DAMERON)

VÉRA AND VN AT THE SHARPS'
HOUSE AT CORNELL WITH THE
SHARPS' CAT, BANDIT.
1958.
(PHOTO: MACLEAN DAMERON)

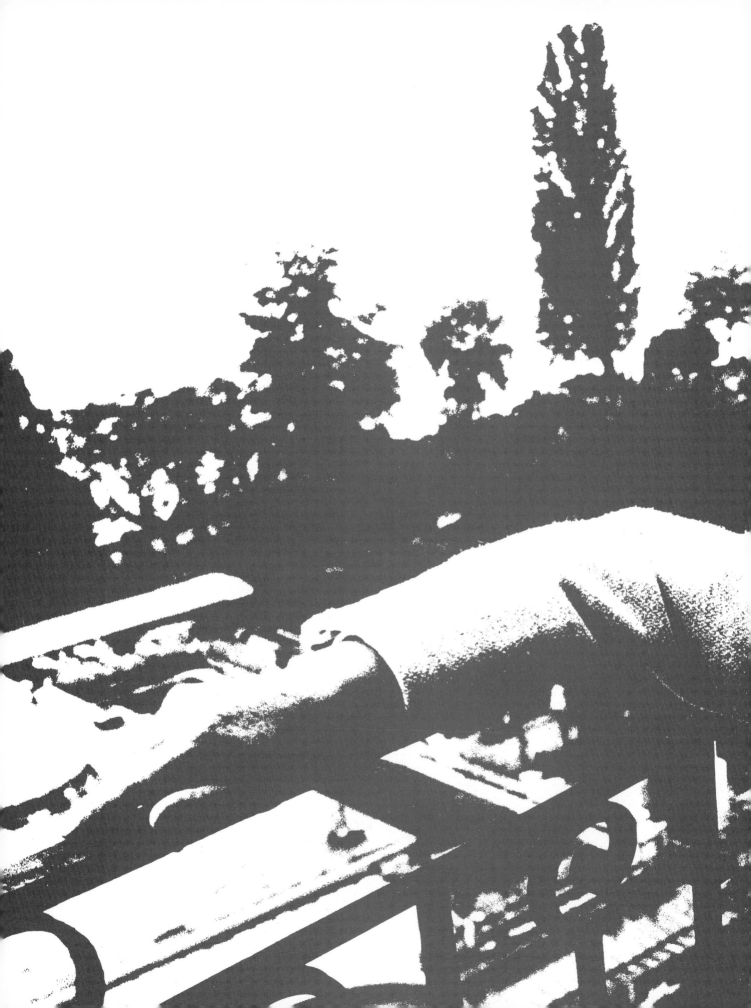

SWITZERLAND

VÉRA (LEFT, FACING CAMERA) AND VN AT THE CELEBRATION FOR THE ITALIAN PUBLICATION OF *LOLITA* BY MONDADORI. MILAN, 1959.

(PHOTO: PATELLANI)

ON THE *QUEEN ELIZABETH*, SOUTHAMPTON, ENGLAND.

NOVEMBER 2, 1960.

Basso **Dmitri Nabokov**

DMITRI IN THE ROLE OF RAIMONDO IN

LUCIA DI LAMMERMOOR,

WITH HIS PARENTS.

REGGIO EMILIA, MAY, 1961.

DMITRI AT THE TIME OF HIS DÉBUT IN

LA BOHÉME.

APRIL, 1961.

VN, 1962.

(PHOTO: HORST TAPPE)

(PHOTO: TOPAZIA MARKEVITCH)

VN ON HIS MONTREUX BALCONY.

(PHOTO: JEAN WALDIS)

VN AND HIS SISTER, ELENA SIKORSKI, AT THE REGGIO EMILIA TRAIN STATION. APRIL, 1961.

VN WITH THE FIRST EDITION OF *PALE FIRE*, 1962. (PHOTO: HORST TAPPE)

VN WRITING AT HIS LECTERN. MONTREUX, 1966.

WRITING ON THE VERANDA OF THE MONTREUX-PALACE HOTEL, 1966. (PHOTO: PHILIPPE HALSMAN)

© *Yvonne Halsman*

BY THE HOTEL POOL, 1966. (PHOTO: PHILIPPE HALSMAN)

© *Yvonne Halsman*

VÉRA AND VN BY THE POOL, 1966. (PHOTO: PHILIPPE HALSMAN)

© *Yvonne Halsman*

SUMMER, 1966. (PHOTO: PHILIPPE HALSMAN)

© Yvonne Halsman

VÉRA AND VN, 1966. (PHOTO: PHILIPPE HALSMAN)

© Yvonne Halsman

VN, 1967. (PHOTO: PHILIPPE HALSMAN)

CHESS ON THE BALCONY. MONTREUX, 1966. (PHOTO: PHILIPPE HALSMAN)

© Horst Tappe

VN ON HIS MONTREUX

BALCONY, 1967.

(PHOTO: HORST TAPPE)

VN, 1970s. (PHOTO: GERTRUDE FEHR)

VN HUNTING BUTTERFLIES ABOVE GSTAAD. SUMMER, 1971. (PHOTO: DMITRI NABOKOV)

VN'S DRAWING OF THE MOUNTAINS NEAR MONTREUX.

AUGUST, 1961.

SAMPLES OF VN'S BUTTERFLY DRAWINGS AS DEDICATIONS.

VN. MONTREUX, 1973.

(PHOTO: R.T. KAHN)

VN, 1970s.

© Elena Seibert

DMITRI NABOKOV. NEW YORK CITY, 1989.

(PHOTO: ELENA SEIBERT)

DMITRI AND VN. LAST KNOWN PHOTOGRAPH. LATE JUNE 1977.

VN DIED ON JULY 2.

VÉRA AND DMITRI AT THE MONTREUX-PALACE HOTEL. MONTREUX, MAY, 1989.

(PHOTO: CLAUDE NABOKOFF)

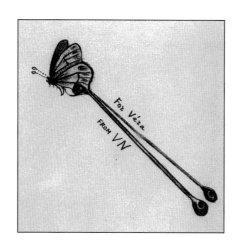